I0463217

For my Wife

Perhaps you wonder where is your bailout after you hear that another bank was rescued by the Government. The same bank that is now calling you few times a day asking for money. The bank that just raised your interest rate because you missed one payment or because maybe they felt like it.

I didn't hear about debt settlement until end of 2008. Some happy speaking guy on the radio commercial was taking about credit card debt, rescue, lowering monthly payments, increasing credit score, you got the idea. It was one of those commercial that you barely listen to, on your way to work early morning each day, trying not to hit the guy in front of you and avoiding being hit by a driver next to your line who thinks that texting and driving can work together. And yes it was one of those commercials where they repeat the phone number three times at the end.

I didn't call the number; I had no need to do that. Of curse I was in debt but, I had nothing to worry about. My wife was working, bills got paid, credit cards payments were current and well above minimum. We were fine. Until our situation changed and our debt got bigger and bigger and when there was no light at the end of the tunnel, a Christmas visit to a friend changed it all.

Part 1: Brief History of getting in to Debt

Before you my reader start to assume that my exaggerated spending got me into debt, then I need you to stop right here. I wasn't shuffling my credit cards like a semi-pro poker player. In fact I was very conservative. If I was going to use credit card I was making sure it got paid at the end of the month so no interest was ever accrued.

My first credit card was from Citibank, and I was proud of it. It had $300.00 secured credit line- that's right- I had to deposit $300 to get it. My credit report was blank and this was a good way to start it. One year later of using the card I got my $300.00 back and a credit line increased to $1000 then $3000 and so after few years I was caring a credit card with $20000 limit. It was nice to think that I could go to the Best Buy and get this brand new fancy computer, but I never developed those habits. If I bought something I hardly paid any interest, if I couldn't pay off the amount at the end of the month I was transferring balances to other credit cards. Having good credit score my mail box was flooded with 0% balance transfers. It was great!

Then my wife got sick and all went down to hill. She had a liver tumor taken out. She is fine now but that cost us a little bit. Then, year later the economy hit the bottom and my pregnant wife was the first one to be "let go" from work. Despite that she had more seniority than other people. Our debt got bigger and bigger, getting close to sixty thousand dollars. We had to do something and fast. Of course before my wife got laid off, we had a plan, simple and effective- get 2nd mortgage and paid off the credit cards. Now we had to do something else.

On a Christmas Eve we went to visit our friend. She is a talker and soon she was telling us that she had over twenty thousands dollars in debt, but she finally have a solution and she can now sleep at night.

"What did you do" I asked

"I called this phone number that I saw on TV. Some company was offering help with credit card debt"

"Help?" That was exactly what we needed. "What kind of help?"

"I setup an account with them. They put me on the plan where I pay them one monthly fee for 3 years and they will take care of my debt." She said smiling.

"So now instead paying $800.00 a month I pay less then $300.

"And they will send that money to the credit card companies? " – That sounded too good to be true. She was going to pay off her twenty something large in 3 years, paying only less then half of it? "How do they do that?"

"I don't know" she said "They work with those banks to cut my payments I guess"

Wrong guess as it turned out. But let me save it for later.

I asked her for the phone number. I was going to call it once we get home.

That's how we found out about

Debt Settlement

How does this works? Simple, you contact you creditor – most likely your credit card company and ask them to accept payment for less the amount own.

Using debt settlement you can cancel your debt by minimum 50%, but most of the time you can get better deal. Especially now (2009) banks will most likely accept much lower %. They know that more people are without the jobs and on the brink of bankruptcy and the last thing the banks wants you to do is go bankrupt. They will loose everything then, so why not accepts 30% and called it a day?

It's sound simple enough but there are few things you must do before banks will even talk to you, and make some other important preparations. I am saying you because you will be the one talking to your creditors. Not your mom or dad or wife or worse- Debt Settlement Company.

Part 2: Getting Ready For Settlement

Gathering Founds

Make sure you will have enough money to offer the settlement. The more the better- it will give you some room to maneuver. Getting at least 50% is a good idea but even if you have 25%-40% that should be enough to get banks interested. You have to have means to save enough money for the settlement, if you don't have it in your budget most likely your only option would be a bankruptcy. Save as much as you can where you can. Buy only things you need, use coupons, cook large meals at home that will last for few days. You don't need to have founds available right now, but you must have them in time for the settlement other wise it will not work! This is something that most Debt Settlement companies will never tell you! They are only interested in their fees.

You will have 180 days or even longer to get them. Why 180 days? Most of the bank will let accounts default for that amount of time. After 180 days of no payment from you the banks can do few things:

- Sell the debt to collection agency
- Take legal action against you – sue
- They will not forget your debt

And even at the 180 day mark, depending on settlement agreement you may have few more months to come up with founds if the settlement is paid in monthly – interest free- installments.

Closing Bank Accounts

If you are going to settle a credit card debt with a bank that is not Federally Chartered (you local banks, credit unions) that you also have a checking or saving account with. Close the account! When the bank sees that you are trying to settle card debt them may invoke:

Right Of Offset Law – and that simply means that they will take what ever is in your bank account to cover the credit card debt. You don't want them to have this option.

Making sure you have the proof of settlement.

Every time you get settlement offer accepted by the bank they need to send you it in writing either by mail or fax.

DO NOT SEND ANY MONEY IF YOU DON"T HAVE IT IN WRITING.

I'll explain in more deeply later on. Getting in trough fax is the best option- most of the banks will do that so make sure you have a fax number ready. If you don't have a fax machine, what you can do is ask your friend or even you can go to KINKOS. Just make sure that you have someone you can trust to pick that fax for you. Look at the confirmation letter I got from Chase. This one was faxed to me.

Cardmember Service
P.O. Box 15548
Wilmington, DE 19886-5548

June 10, 2009

Pawel Z Czajkowski

**Important information is
provided below regarding
your account.**

RE: Your account ending in ▆▆▆

Dear Pawel Z Czajkowski:

We are pleased to confirm that we've agreed to settle your credit card account for $2874. Our settlement brings you these three advantages:

- You will pay 2874, a significant savings over the full balance that you owe us*.
- We will stop all efforts to collect.
- We will report your account to the national credit bureaus as "settled"*.

Here is your schedule of payments that you have agreed to:

	Due Date		Payment Amount	
First Installment:	06/18/2009		Payment Amount:	$2874
Second Installment:	Due Date:		Payment Amount:	$
Third Installment:	Due Date:		Payment Amount:	$
Fourth Installment:	Due Date:		Payment Amount:	$

Please call 1-866-560-9081 toll-free to make payment arrangements, or you can mail us your payment to the address below. For your convenience, your first payment due will be given a 10-day grace period from the due date listed above. We must receive your payment before your grace period expires, or before the date your account is scheduled to charge off, whichever comes first. If you have any questions about your settlement agreement or, want to find out your charge off date, please call us at 1-866-560-9081.

Until your settlement amount is paid in full, your Annual Percentage Rate will be 14.99%. This will have no impact on your settlement amount or payment(s). If you don't make each required payment by its due date listed above, including any applicable grace period, we receive an insufficient payment or your payment is returned for insufficient funds (NSF) our settlement agreement will terminate and your account will revert to the terms of your Cardmember Agreement. If you are removed from the settlement plan, we'll continue our collection efforts and any payments made to that point

Account is owned by Chase Bank USA, N.A.
Calls may be monitored and/or recorded to ensure the highest level of quality service.

PP0015

Continued

Another good way of tracking settlement is to record all your conversation with the bank. If you live in One Party State you don't have to inform the person you are talking to as long as the other person also lives in One Party State. If the other person is in Two Party State then you need informed him/or her that you are recording. Here is the list of states that allow One Party:

Alaska

Arkansas

Colorado

District of Columbia

Georgia

Hawaii

Idaho

Indiana

Iowa

Kansas

Kentucky

Louisiana

Maine

Minnesota

Mississippi

Missouri

Nebraska

Nevada

New Jersey

New Mexico

New York

North Carolina

North Dakota

Ohio

Oklahoma

Oregon

Rhode Island

South Carolina

South Dakota

Tennessee

Texas

Utah

Vermont

Virginia

West Virginia

Wisconsin

Wyoming

And list of Two Part States

California

Connecticut

Delaware

Florida

Illinois

Maryland

Massachusetts

Michigan

Montana

New Hampshire

Pennsylvania

You can use hand held recorder or, if you have a computer you will need a program that can record sounds and microphone.

Choosing a way to pay for Settlement

Once you reach settlement with bank then you need to send a payment. The best way to do it is to send money order or cashier check. Sometimes bank may insist on payment over the phone. If you choose this route – NEVER and I mean NEVER give them your regular checking bank account number. For the purpose of settlement either setup new account or buy a prepaid debit card. Tell the bank, that you need few days to deposit the requested amount and they can debit you account on such and such date. Keep only the exact amount in the account. You don't want them to take more than they should.

When the payment is schedule you should have agreement in writing so there is no understating how much should be paid. But of curse "mistakes" do happen.

Remember, you need to have it black and white. This probably the most important thing when negotiating debt. If you don't have the terms of the settlement on the paper then when you make the payment, bank may refuse to take it as paid in full and you still will be obligated to pay the rest. Worse, your account will be current again and you will have to start the whole process again, incurring more interest and late fee.

Stop using your credit cards

This should be probably the first thing on the list. No more credit cards. You want to get ride of debt not to incur more of it.

Stop paying your cards

You heard it right. In order to get bank attention you need to stop making payments.

Credit card companies will not talk to you if you are current on you cards. Why would they? There is no problem. They are still getting paid according to the terms and conditions of the card agreement. They have no reason to lower your debt. When I called HSBC and asked about settling my credit card with them, I was told politely that this is not possible at the moment;

"When it is going to be possible form to settle the debt then?" I asked

"The account must be at least 90 days past due for us to consider debt settlement" The rep responded.

"Great! I'll call back later"

And I did called two months later and was able to negotiate the settlement.

Now, what will happen when you stop sending payments? Just the usual:

- The bank will increase interest rate
- The bank will slam you with late fee
- Your credit score will suffer

- Your credit card may get frozen- this is actually good thing because you won't be able to use it. No that you wanted to anyway.

- The bank may – and this is my favorite – reduce your credit limit so your credit card is now maximized and every later fee will now "earn" you Over Limit Fee.

- The bank may also sue you or send your credit card to collection agency – but this is highly unlikely giving fact that most of banks will wait 180 days before taking any legal action. Think about it. How many people are later each month? Do they get sued? No. It simple not cost effective to do that from the bank perspective.

So this is what could happen to you, more or less when you stop making payments. Believe me there is no other way. What bank may you offer though, is some hardship plan that will last 3-12 months with lowered interested so you can catch up. If you believe that you will some how come in position of enough money to pay your debt during that plan- take it. If not, once the plan ends you will be back at square one. And this is not what you want. You want to get ride of debt.

Part 3: Debt Settlement and Credit Score

What is going to happen to your Credit Score

Have you heard about Titanic? The greatest ship of it's time struck an iceberg and sunk to the bottom of the Atlantic like a rock. This is exactly what is going to happen to your credit score. Two negative things will cause this:

- No payment
- Settling for less than full balance

In other words debt settlement has the same affect on your credit report as bankruptcy does; it will stay there for seven years affecting your credit score. But look at this on a bright side. If you have $10000.00 in debt, paying only minimum will take you years to pay it off and you will pay much, much more in interest. Most of us who went debt settlement road had much larger debt than $10000, I had almost 65 thousand! My credit score was over 720 but it was the last thing on my mind. I could care less about it as long as I'm debt free and can sleep at night. And if you have a large debt chances are, your score is already low, so what are you worry about?

The score will go down and no bank will land me any money, I won't be able to buy a care or a house. Can I now? With 65000 in debt and over a thousand dollars in monthly minimum payment I can't buy anything anyway. But once I'm done with settlement my credit score will improve and after 7 years I will have high score again.

If not for the settlement I would be probably paying my 65K debt to the day I die, at 29% interest rate! What you may not know, there is a lot more to your credit then just a score. There is this thing called Debt to Income Ratio. So if someone has 75%-80% DTI ratio but is current on his loans and credit card and has a high credit score of 730 – I was that person – does not necessary means that she or he will be able to get another loan. As a matter of fact a person with debt to income ratio 20%-25% and few missed payments in the past is more likely to get a loan.

Fortunately once you are out of debt your score will start to go up and you will start getting new credit card offers in the mail and after seven years the negative information from report will be removed.

My score is now 664 – six months after the settlement. Not bad. I was expecting it to be at 400 levels. What a nice surprise! Once the debt is gone you actually have more buying power than the person that sill have large balance on the credit card, because you are not making any monthly payments. Just make sure you stay out of debt this time.

Part 4: Settling the debt with original creditor

The first 3 months.

If you did what said in Part 2 then all you have to do is wait few months. During that time banks will call you on daily basis. Sometimes 5-6 times as day – per bank! When we were doing settlement I had 12-15 calls a day. It is good idea to have a separate phone for those calls and make sure it's not your work phone.

When they call for the first 2 months don't bother talking to them. All they want is to let you know that you are late on your credit card – like you don't know that already. And they want you to make a payment. Now, this important part. Do not send any money at this point. This will only reset the "waiting period" of you settlement back to zero days and you will have to start all over again. At least 3 months need to pass without payment before banks will start any settlement talk. You will of course incur late fees and over limit fees (if you are over limit) and the fastest you reach 120-150 day mark the better.

The probability that the bank will sue you before 180 dead line is highly unlikely. What they will do thought, is to try to scare you, intimidate you with letters and phone calls. Look at the letter I received from HSBC.

Account Number:	████████
Card Type:	████
Account Balance:	$3,216.99
Status:	31 Days Past Due
Amount Due:	$166.00
Submit By:	04/07/2009

***************MIXED AADC 430
Pawel Czajkowski
██████████
████████████

03/23/2009

IT IS TIME FOR YOU TO MAKE A CRITICAL DECISION ABOUT YOUR MENARDS ACCOUNT THAT COULD AFFECT YOUR CREDIT.

Dear Pawel Czajkowski:

Your MENARDS Account is currently 31 days past due and may have been reported to the credit bureaus as delinquent. It is time for you to make a decision:

You can either act now to resolve this problem or do nothing and risk additional damage to your credit that could take years to repair.

It's not too late, but time is limited. We are ready to work with you to find a mutually agreeable solution.

We understand situations exist that make it difficult to pay debts in a timely manner. That is why it is important that you contact us before 04/07/2009.

Make your payment of $166.00 by 04/07/2009 by contacting us at www.hrsaccount.com/menards or by mailing the coupon below with your check. If you need other assistance or cannot make the payment today, call me immediately at 1-877-652-4023.

If I do not hear from you by 04/07/2009, we may proceed with other collection options.

The worst thing you could do at this point is nothing.

Sincerely yours,

Michelle Sorvillo
Unit Manager, Collections Department

P.S. Make your payment of $166.00 by 04/07/2009 at www.hrsaccount.com/menards or by mailing the coupon below so we can work together on a solution. If you need further assistance or cannot make the payment today, call me immediately at 1-877-652-4023.

 www.hrsaccount.com/menards   1-877-652-4023   Payment Processing Center
PO Box 4144
Carol Stream, IL 60197-9195

HSBC Card Services Inc., and/or HSBC Card Services (II) Inc., and/or HSBC Private Label Corporation, affiliates of HSBC Bank Nevada, N.A. (the issuer of this Account), provide administrative and processing services for this credit card or line of credit program.
This is an attempt to collect a debt and any information obtained will be used for that purpose. MCC-HH-RM-F 0209

It sounds like it is a last call, if I do not act now all hell will break loose. The letter was from April and I later settled this account in July. I was not sued, my balance was not sold to collection agency and no one showed up at my door. I simply received another phone call and another letter.

I don't know if you know this or not, but the letters and phone calls are not sent by people but by automated system. The computer knows who is late on the credit card and run appropriate program that generates the later. No one even is folding them or closing the envelope. All is done by the machine. Even the phone calls are dialed by a computer. When you pick up the phone and say "hello" the computer on the other line hears that sound and then connects you with a live person.

Best way to deal with collection calls made by a machine is to let the machine answered them. I had to clear my voice mail box every 2-3 days at some time. You can answer the phone call and talk to the customer service, but most likely they are not calling to offer you settlement, they are calling to ask for payment. Remember few pages back about my phone call to HSBC? They literally told me to wait longer.

While the phone is ringing start to think of you debt story for the customer service. In my case it was simple; wife had major surgery, and then lost her job. This could have happened to everybody and most of you have similar stories. Make sure you tell them that when you call. Most likely they will ask you themselves what drove you into debt. Don't tell them your life story. Few sentences that's all what is needed. AND I don't have to tell to avoid saying things like:

"I though it would be cool to have this 58" plasma TV for $7000 in my bedroom."

Although yes, it would be great to have it, it just not going to work. You have to be serious and professional. Also don't make any threats. I know it is tempting to say;

"You got your bailout, and where is mine?"

Or

"My tax money has helped you, why can't you help me?"

I thought of saying that at first but I didn't. Although it is truth, it would only make the other person on the line angry and not willing to help you at all. You need to know that the people of customer service are people just like you and me with their own sets of problem and debts. The last thing they want to hear is someone who needs help screaming at them. And it's not like they are the one who needed bailout. It was their CEO who will still get his multimillion dollar bonus.

So remember, no yelling, no threats, no raising voice, no fast talking. Just tell your story in calm, professional way. And because the times are though, millions of people filling bankruptcy, most banks are prepared to accept settlement; they will just negotiate the %. And you want it to get as low as possible. When you call, you may even not tell your story, you just say that you want to settle your outstanding amount for X amount of $ and the customers service representative may say yes to it. When I called Chase for the first time after 4 months, I said exactly that. I offered 25%, they counter offered with 30%. I said fine, done deal. The phone was no longer than 10 minutes- not including hold time of course! I was pleasantly surprised how easy it was, my confidence grew and settling the rest of the debt was relatively easy as well.

No matter what banks tell or ask, you want one thing – settle the debt. Have answer prepared for their questions and counter offers they will repeat them probably as often as possible.

4th and 5th month into settlement

Three months has passed it is now over 100 days when you sent last payment. The phone is still ringing and you mail box is full of "remind" letters. Your settlement founds should also be growing unless of course you had the money from the beginning. At this point it is a good idea to visit a bankruptcy lawyer. That's right you read it correctly. Find a local lawyer and call for a meeting. Most of them will not charge you a fee for consultations but even if you have to spend $200 that will be worth it.

In case your settlement does not go as planned – it can happen – you will have to look at other options to get ride of debt. When you talk to this lawyer, just talk about bankruptcy in general. Mention that you are doing or thinking about debt settlement but don't go into details. Get his business card.

This meeting may help you get better settlement. Your credit card banks do not want you to declare bankruptcy. They are afraid of it. They will loose everything if you do that so why not take 25 cent on the dollar? Or 30? They will be more willing to accept your settlement offer if they know that you are already talking to bankruptcy lawyer and if they ask you the name and phone number of the attorney. Give it to them. Let them verify that you are serious.

It's now the time to contact each your creditors and start to negotiate.

Wait for the end of the month and call them. Last week of the month is the best. Use the number from the letters that were sent to you over the past months. These phone number are better then those listed on you credit cards. Most often the numbers are for collection department within the bank-not a collection agency.

You will be required to provide the standard info:

- Name
- Account number
- Last 4 digits of you social security number
- Security question if any

After you gave the above, eight of ten times the first thing they say is that your account is seriously past due and if you would like to make a payment to bring it current.

You answer is **no**.

Tell them you want to settle the balance for a dollar amount.

Most banks will settle between 20-40%, the closer to the charge off date the better but you may get great deal weeks before that. Don't be afraid to ask when the charge off date is.

When you talk to the bank don't tell them that you offer them – let's just say – 30%. Use the dollar amount and let them figure out the %. You will have that ready on your side. When you offer fixed $ they will think that this is the only money you have – and most likely it is. Also do not tell them that this is your money saved under the carpet. They will ask you where the money will come from. Your answer should be – family sources, don't tell them you going to borrow from another bank because that's just silly and they won't believe that. No financial institution is going to lend you any money anyway. Pay day loans are also without questions. Family source is the safest way.

Offer them at first 20%-25% even if you have money to settle at 40%. Leave yourself room to negotiate.

When I was ready to call I called Bank of America and after providing initial info I said:

"I would like to settle my balance for $X

Their response:

"I'm sorry but the lowest we could do is 30%"

And that was maybe 2 minutes into the conversation. I agreed to it because it was within my goal.

Chase was exactly the same. I was able to settle four credit cards in 45 minutes! And it took that "long" because I was on hold most of the time.

It is unlikely that at this point in time the bank will say that they do not offer the settlements. If they don't, that means they are trying to intimidate you. Don't worry. Politely say fine, goodbye and hung up. Call them again few days later using the same phone number or different one. You most likely get different person on the phone.

If they do offer settlement but they offer 50% – 70%, tell them that you do not have that much money and politely end the conversation. Remember be polite, the people you talk to, record all the conversation and also put notes in their system. Call them again in few days.

In my case Bank of America and Chase settled fast, but HSBC and Citibank were plying hard. I had to call them few times and it took me 7 more weeks to finally bring the settlement amount within my goal.

If the bank does not accept your offer, try asking what you have to do make them accept it. Trust me it may work. When I called HSBC on one of my accounts it was close to 90 days past due, the lady I talk to was super nice and she said that accounts need to be over 90 days past due for settlement. Sometimes they may tell you that the account needs to go trough 2 more stages before they can accept any settlements. Now, the longer the account is past the better chance that you get best offer.

They may also tell you that once the account is past 180 days it will be marked as "charge off" and send to a different department where you can call and get lower % rate.

You may also wait until 180 days are up if you not going anywhere with the offer. If the person you talk to is rude and demanding – hung up and do not call them for couple of days, also do not pick up phone calls from them let the machine take care of it. When the time is right they will either send you an offer in the mail or you call them again after few days of silence. They will be more willing to talk.

"In my case, Chase settled for 25% for a ~20K balance, just a few days before charge off. They had initially declined to settle at all, and then offered 70%, then 50%, followed by 40% and finally 25%."

When I was doing all the research about debt settlement, I wondered if banks have special people – let's called them alpha teams – whos only job was to scare and intimidate people in debt in order to accept what the bank was offering. I think they do.

Also do not fall statements that say for example:

"If you do not make $X payment now the whole amount would be due."

Or

"You account will be sent to outside collection agency if we do not receive payment"

Before 180 days are up it is unlikely that the bank will do anything to your account apart from adding interest and late fees. Unless of curse you hired a debt settlement company, but if you followed my advice from the beginning of this book you didn't.

If you have all the funds for the settlement, tell them that you will pay in one lump sum. This way bank can agree to better deal because they may offer 30% in lump sum or 50% in four payments. If not tell them, that you will pay them in few installments. My settlement with Citibank was made in three, interest free payments because I did not have the entire amount.

"I offered Chase a 35% settlement twice and was denied both times. Then a rep finally told me I was wasting my time until my account got to the 120-140 day mark. At 140 days they took 40% over 90 days. They offered to take 35% if I could pay lump sum"

You can, but that maybe hard to accomplish, try to negotiate with the bank that you only pay what was the original amount of credit before you stopped making payments.

That means that you are not going to pay for the late, over limit fess and interest. You may be able to cancel fees but the interest will be hard to pull off. Since you stopped paying you credit card bills, depending on your total debt you could have additional few hundred if not thousand of dollars to pay off. You need to take that under consideration when accepting offers from the bank.

What is a 50% now, was 35% few months ago. I had an offer like that from Chase which I had to reject.

CHASE

P.O. Box 2188 • Westport, CT 06880-0188

CHASE SETTLEMENT PLAN

Balance as of 06/02/2009:	WE'LL ACCEPT:
$14,229.95	$7,115.00

AMOUNT YOU SAVE:
$7,115.00

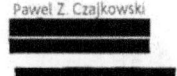

Pawel Z. Czajkowski
[redacted]

EXPIRES:
06/18/2009

Limited-time offer. Call 1-888-809-0194 immediately.

When you accept this settlement and pay the reduced amount shown, we will stop all collection calls.

Lighten your load. Pay a reduced amount and we'll finalize your debt.

Dear Pawel Z. Czajkowski,

It's not too late to make a very smart decision – one that can take a considerable weight off your shoulders.

Settle your account for good.

With our simple Chase settlement plan, you have a great opportunity to put your outstanding credit card balance behind you once and for all. Best of all, you can do it for a lot less than what you owe.

As the attached coupon shows, we will accept a reduced payment of at least $7,115.00 if you respond by the date above. When you pay this amount, we'll stop any collection calls immediately and we will report your account as settled to the credit reporting agencies upon completion of your settlement. Payments or credits in excess of this amount will be applied against your entire outstanding balance.

We'll meet you part way. But you must act now.

When your account is past due, it's falling behind with each passing day, even if you don't hear from us. If you do nothing or wait too long, you'll miss out on this special opportunity. If that happens, you'll once again be responsible for the full amount owed.

One phone call is all it takes.

Wouldn't it feel great to resolve your balance, and have one less bill to worry about? Call us today at 1-888-809-0194 to make payment arrangements. Or, simply talk to us about your situation and get it off your chest. Odds are, we have a way to help you get the weight off your shoulders.

Sincerely,

A. Gordon Dennis

A. Gordon Dennis
Customer Support Manager

P.S. Very Important: Even if you don't think a settlement offer is right for you, there are other ways we can help. Call us today at 1-888-809-0194. We'll be glad to discuss other payment solutions that can help you resolve your debt.

We are required by the IRS to provide information about certain amounts that are discharged as a result of a cancellation of a debt on a form 1099C. If we are required to notify the IRS, you will receive a copy of the form 1099C that is filed with the IRS.
Account is owned by Chase Bank USA, N. A. Calls may be monitored and/or recorded to ensure the highest level of quality service.

I need to mention that when I use word negotiate, it literally means to repeat your debt story, your offer –what you can and cannot afford- over and over again. Sometimes you are going to find yourself talking like a broken vinyl record. Just be polite, speak slowly and try not to change your tone or raise your voice. If they are rude – hang up. They will hang up if you are rude. But because you, the taxpayer rescued the banks, there is a high chance that they will offer you settlement right away.

Once the dollar amount is agreed on by both sides, ask for the terms in writing. You have to have it in writing before you send payment! You can of course send check without it, but do it on your own risk.

If you have fax number ready ask bank to fax it to you. That way you can send payment next day and be debt free faster. If you don't have fax, tell bank to mail you the terms of settlement. Sometimes you may be told that they do not send or fax settlement offers. This is a lie.

When I called Chase and they agree to settle for 30%, I was told that they can't fax me the offer because they just don't do that;

"But if I send you payment you may back out on the agreement and then I won't be able to prove that my account was settled" – I said

Their response:

"We will not back out and all the phone calls are recorded"

Sure they are. But people have short memory and the phone records can be deleted. I did not wanted to loose this great offer, so I said fine and hang up. I knew that if the guy was telling the truth, he put all the settlement details in the system regarding my account and all I had to do is to call Chase again using different number, talk different customer service representative and ask him or her to fax me the offers. I did just that and 30 minutes I had them in my hand. I don't know if the first person was lazy or just having a bad day. The truth is, they all have access to fax machines and they can send the settlement agreement with little or no trouble.

Sometimes bank will only fax you the settlement agreement if you give them the account number from which they will draw the settlement money. Some banks will accept checks but some will take only wire transfer. In my case Bank of America and Citibank insisted on that and I said fine. Just make sure when this is the case, to have separate account ready with no money in it. You only put money and only the exact amount the day before the payment date!

In some rare cases even if you receive the settlement offer in the mail or trough the fax machine, bank may refuse to accept it. This happens very rare.

"I did a settlement in 3 payments and the last payment I went to pay yesterday. But they said that they are sorry but they never do a settlement for 25percent and 40 percent is the lowest offered. She said the lady that did it shouldn't have and it's not a settlement that they allow. It is Bank of America who did it but FIA letter head is on my agreement."

If it is your first payment – don't pay it. If you paying in installments, and already paid some – ask for refund. If it was lump sum and you send the money – too bad for

them – the settlement is done and they can't do anything about it. You could sue the bank for breach of contract if they do not accept the settlement provided that you have it in writing.

In the above case most likely bank made an error and offered 25% on the account that was only 2-3 months past due. Most of the time however the settlement goes trough and Bank of America is the easiest to work with.

Conclusion

That's all there is to it. As you can see this is not that hard. I know it is tough to listen to those phone ringing, people asking for payments, but in order for the settlement to work you have to overcome it. I was afraid too when I made my first phone call to the bank. I did not know what to expect. Are they going to yell at me? Are they going to say no and not listen to me at all? It turns out that it was rather the opposite, everybody I talked to was super nice! Fact, some banks are tougher than others but it also depends on the person you are talking too, and since there is a lot of customer service reps working in the bank you may get a really nice person that will make your day. Not even one person was mean to me or made me angry. Settling my debt was a really great experience and despite the reputation that our nation Banks have, they do offer help to consumers and we should not be afraid to ask them for it.

Look at the Bank of America settlement offer I was able to negotiate.

www.bankofamerica.com

PAWEL Z CZAJKOWSKI

▮▮▮▮▮▮▮▮▮▮

June 11, 2009

Account No.: ▮▮▮▮▮▮▮▮

Dear Pawel Z Czajkowski:

This letter outlines our conversation regarding a proposal to settle the above-referenced account. You can save 70% by settling your account. This is a savings of $13,784.21. To take advantage of this offer you must call 1.800.606.3376, Monday through Friday 8 a.m. - 9 p.m. or Saturday 8 a.m. - 12 p.m.. to initiate the first payment. Each additional installment is listed below.

Settlement Installment	Installment Due Date
$6,000.00	June 25, 2009

By completing this payment plan, your account will be considered settled, and you will not be obligated to pay the remaining balance, provided no additional charges appear on this account after the date of this letter. Also, any future account activity that results in a credit balance will become the property of FIA Card Services, N.A. Any violation of this agreement will result in the full outstanding balance of $19,784.21 being due immediately. All payments must be received by the installment due dates listed above.

If the remaining amount is equal to or greater than $600.00, we are required by federal law (IRS section 6050P) to report this amount. You will be receiving a Form 1099-C from FIA Card Services, N.A. no later than next January 31st. If you have any questions regarding your personal taxes, we recommend that you consult a certified public accountant or other tax professional.

If I, poor immigrant from Eastern Europe could do this, you can too! Good luck!

Now let me vent, because what really makes me angry are

Part 5: Debt Settlement Companies

Hell No!

You can hire debt settlement company to handle your debt, but please don't! This probably the worst decision you could make. Why? Because they don't do anything that you could do yourself plus they will charge thousands of dollars for their "service" and most of the time they will leave you in worst shape than before.

When I was researching debt settlement I though of hiring Debt Settlement Company. It was my first though, especially after my friend did the same and she had her payments reduced. I was ready to actually print the contract, sign it and fax it to one of those companies, with my all personal and payment information. Luckily for the reason me unknown the printer refused to work that day (I'm a computer geek by the way) , I decided to print the contract at work. Next day while driving I had a though;

"Maybe I should research a little bit more before I spent few thousands on somebody who says things too good to be true."

And I found that yes – debt settlement works – but debt settlement companies don't.

Who ever though about debt settlement LLC business model was a con artist genius. Maybe in the beginning it was though as a great way to help people, but in time it evolved into something completely opposite.

Almost all DSC will promise you this:

- Lower your payments
- Stop collection calls
- Negotiate debt on your behalf
- Experience in settling debt
- Trained negotiators
- Knowledge in consumer law and in
- Fair Credit Reporting Act (FCRA) and Fair Debt Collection Practices Act (FDCPA),

Here how it works;

Lowered Payments

The payments are not lowered. I know, in their advertising it sounds like they contact your banks and ask for payment reduction. That is not the case. In order for the debt settlement to work you have to save % of your debt so you can offered it to your creditors as a payment in full. So the DSC will setup and "account" for you called "reserve" and they will put there the money you pay them each month. Usually it is much less what you used to pay for your credit cards. What they don't tell you or they will tell that this is ok, is that for the first few months 4-6 or longer, most of the money you send will go to their fees, leaving little or no money in your reserve account. So for example if you pay debt Settlement Company a month $500, only $100 or less may go to the reserve account, the rest is kept by the company as fee

for their "help". On top of that there maybe additional administrative fees.

Why do they do that? Why do they collect their fees first? Because they know that you, the debtor have only 180 days since last credit card payment to settle the debt and since they put you in their 36 or so monthly plan that upon completion you will have enough money to settle the debt.

What bank in the World will wait 36 months for their money?! Not one! The original creditor will sell your debt to a collection agency for a profit while they write off the debt as a loss and get some money and yes, if the debt stays there for the 36 months you may have a chance to settle the debt, but then what collection agency in the World will wait 36 or so months for the money? Not one! They will most likely sue you.

Debt settlement companies know that and that's why they collect their fees first. Once your time is up and you are sued – you are on your own. They will not help you, and the fess? Non-refundable.

If the company collects their fess after the settlement, then yes, it would be helpful to use it and you could settle some debts, providing that you saved enough money in your reserve account.

When you hire debt Settlement Company you are also more likely to be sued by the creditors. Why? Because the creditor also knows how the DSC works and instead sending your credit card payments to them you are paying someone else! **Come on!!!**

Almost all of the people who enrolled in to those so called debt settlement programs dropped out. According to National Consumer Law Center only 1.4% completed it. The rest drops out after incurring fees.

"DO NOT GO WITH <removed name>. They definitely misrepresent. The program was not at all what they told me it would be. I went into their program two years ago and I have quit it because I am in much worse shape than I was when I joined. And I now have a 2nd lawsuit against me. I have had to file bankruptcy. I was trying to do the right thing (or so I thought) by going with a debt settlement company instead of filing bankruptcy. All that did was take my money and now I have to file bankruptcy anyway. DO NOT LET THEM TALK YOU INTO THIS PROGRAM"

Stopping Collection Calls

Once you stop paying credit cards you will be receiving collection calls few times a day. Debt settlement companies claim they can stop collection calls. They do this by sending "Cease and Desist" letter to the creditor and/or sometimes they will provide you with a blank form which you will have to fill out and send it yourself – and this is why you pay your monthly fee remember?

Well, the stop collection letter will work on collection agency but not for the bank who tries to collect its own debt. This is because; the federal fair debt collection law and most state laws cover third party debt collectors only and not the original creditor. Here is the exact wording from the contract I pulled from one of those "miracle" debt relief companies that you have to sign when hiring them:

"Your creditors may continue collection efforts on delinquent accounts. Such collection efforts can include phone calls and letters to you, charging off the account, sending accounts to collection agencies or

attorneys, lawsuits and even garnishments of your wages if a judgment has been obtained. "

Did you hear the same thing over the phone when you talk to them? I don't think so. They make it sound so great that, rarely anyone reads the contract. So much for stopping collection calls.

So the phone will still be ringing and when you tell that to your debt settlement company, they will tell you to either ignore it or answer the phone and instructed the person on the other side to contact you debt Settlement Company. And when you do just that guess what bank knows now? That you hired a debt settlement company and now they may sue you or send your account to collection even before the 180 days are up.

Negotiate debt on your behalf

But the Debt Settlement Company will start to negotiate your debt with your creditor only after you have sufficient money in your "reserve" account. And how much money you have there after few months? Most likely very little because you are still paying fees.

"I have been with <Name Removed> for 18 months, and so far they have taken over $17,000 in fees for only settling @ $40,000 in debt. I have been sued by 3 debtors so far, and more is yet to come, even though I signed up with them to AVOID all the blood, sweat and tears that come with fighting creditors in court. I have had to settle thousands of dollars of debt OUT OF MY OWN POCKET, yet they are still retaining all fees collected!!!!"

Some of the companies don't even bother to contact the creditors to negotiate the settlement; they may tell that they do but in fact all they care is to collect their fee as soon as possible before you drop out. And they know you will 98.6% at the time. They are actually counting on you being sued by the creditors, because that way they don't have to do anything.

They will not help you when you are taken to the court even if the Debt Settlement Company has a "Law" word in its name. Nine out of ten they are not or don't employ lawyers!

Experience in settling debt

Most of the settlement companies claim that they have long and established relationship with creditors and they know who they need to contact and how they need to talk. This is a lie. Most creditors will say that do not work with debt settlement companies because of privacy and other issues. They have no "special relationships" with banks or creditors as they claim, at least not anymore than you do. During my research I found one company that claimed to gather debts from multiple individuals into packets and then approaching creditors. Supposedly that way they can negotiate better settlement from creditors. What a bunch of crap.

Trained negotiators

They only have trained sales people whose only job is convince people to sign up. Some of them even play approval game. You fill out and applications and they will call you back to let you know if you were approved or not. 99.9999% at the time you are approved. Some will tell you that banks will not talk to you and therefore you can't settle or your own. They will sell you all kinds of bullshit just to make you sign up and start sending payments. Don't believe me? Try it. Call one of those

companies and see for yourself. Don't tell them any personal info and if you can call from phone booth or from internet phone. That way they won't know who is calling.

And what they can tell the creditor you cannot tell your self? No much really. Worst, they can be rude, demanding, alienating and this is not the way to get creditor to settle. This is actually a good way to have the account sent to collection sooner or get sued. What I said during negotiating with my banks was my debt story and what I can afford or not. That's it. There was no movie talk 50 – 20, 45- 25.

And most of those people who work at the debt Settlement Companies work there for very short time, because the company will either be closed by State attorney or they will quit because they discover it is nothing but a scam. If they are trained, then the only thing I can think of is that they are trained to read the script.

Knowledge in consumer law and in Fair Credit Reporting Act (FCRA) and Fair Debt Collection Practices Act (FDCPA)

Please, this sounds like all the people that are negotiating your debt are lawyers. If you decided somehow to talk to one of these companies and they tell you that they know the law or that they have attorney on staff, ask for that attorney license number. Let them surprised you!

"The person that called me sounded like a kid and when I asked him a legal question he responded by saying, "I can't answer or give you any legal advice, because I'm not a Lawyer!" (HUH???) "So why did you called me I asked him" and he's response was to tell me to get a LAWYER!!! Because they can't represent me in a court of law!! So, I have paid <Name Removed> $618.00 monthly for the past 8 months which adds up to $4,944 ... ... in total $4,312 went to them and $632 is in escrow so they can't even negotiate with the creditor that is suing me because I don't have enough in escrow!!"

The above is another sad and true story of how a debt relief company can rip you off and leave in worse financial shape than before you joined up the debt settlement program. My friend from the beginning of this book end up being sued by the collection agency, she cancelled her debt settlement program and fill out a police report. Did she get her money back? No. This is another reason why these companies operate. It is hard to get your money back. Even if you try to sue them it will take time and money and the people who are scammed don't have either. Your only option is to fill out complain with Federal Trade Commission and your state Attorney General. If enough complaints are filled, the FTC will take action. Here is an example taken directly from Federal Trade Commission press release:

"Four debt-negotiation companies have agreed to settle Federal Trade Commission charges that they violated federal law by falsely claiming they could reduce consumers' debt by up to 60 percent, leading many people into financial ruin and bankruptcy. The proposed settlements bar them from engaging in further violations of the Federal Trade Commission Act.

The settling defendants were among three individuals and seven companies charged by the FTC with deceptive and unfair practices in violation of the FTC Act. All of the defendants in the nationwide operation were charged with misrepresenting how much they could reduce consumers' debt, and not adequately disclosing the likelihood that consumers would be sued if they took the defendants' advice and stopped paying creditors. The FTC also charged the defendants with not disclosing that consumers' account balances would grow from interest, interest rate increases, late fees, and other charges; and falsely advising

consumers that negative information that appeared on their credit report as a result of participating in the defendants' program would be removed upon completion of the program."

Go to http://ftc.gov/opa/2008/09/nss.shtm to read the full article.

And why would you want to hire debt Settlement Company in the first place? Almost all creditors will settle with for just taking to them! Some will send you the settlement offer without any action from you. If they don't, they will maybe offer different options like hardship programs or lower interest payment plans for FREE! My only cost of the settlement (not including the late fees and interest on the credit cards) was around $20 for printing cashier checks and mailing them registered mail.

Debt settlement companies on the other hand will charge you thousands of dollars for their "service". They take their cut from the beginning called setup and administration fees. With all these fees it is hard to save up money for the potential settlement because little or no funds are deposited to the reserve account until the set-up fees are paid in full.

Some will also have account maintenance fee. Almost all will charge you the percentage of the amount saved by them ranging from 10% to 25%. For example they settled an account with balance of $1000 for 50%. So they saved you 500.00 now, if they take 15% of the saved amount $500 X 15% that's $75 for them. Even if you settle with creditor on your own but still was enrolled in their "program" they will take their cut.

To better see the picture let's use my example. I had $65000.00 in debt. If the debt settlement company could settle my debt at the same rate as I did – 35% on average they would have saved me $42250.00

The company that I was going to sing up with was taking $3000 up front setup fee and 20% of the saved amount:

$3000 + 20% * $42250.00 = $11450.00

That's how much I would have paid them, assuming that they would actually perform the service they advertise which is highly unlikely they will. So instead settling at 35% my settlement would be at 52%. Still less than the full $65000 but I settled on my own and did not have to pay anybody.

They will also tell you that the creditor will not settle with you or that you won't be able to handle the rude talk and the tactics that the creditor will use on you to get paid. This is not true. All the people I talked to get the settlement done were super nice and very helpful. All of them offered help of some sort including the settlement. For them it's actually against the law to threat the debtor. Banks will not do that, if they do they will be in serious trouble.

Not all however Debt Relief Companies are bad. There are some good ones. If you decided to hire some one to handle your debt, make sure that they charge you a service fee **AFTER** the settlement, never before.

Collection agencies may however use illegal tactics to collect the money.

Part 6: Settling the debt with collection agency

When 180 days are up and you did not reach settlement or you just simply had not enough money to attempt one, bank will most likely write off the debt as loss and get a tax deductions, then it will sell it the debt to the collection agency for as little as 10 cent on the dollar.

The collection agency will then try to collect the debt. They could be ruthless and they don't talk nicely so the best way to communicate with them is not to talk to them over the phone. As soon as you are contacted by CA, usually by phone, tell them that from now on you wanted to be contacted only by mail. That's not enough – to enforced that you have to sent the Cease and Desist letter (see sample below) registered mail return receipt.

Your Name
Your Address
Your Phone#

Collector's Name
Collector's Address
Date

Dear Collection Manager,

Re: Account Number_____

This letter is a written request asking you to cease and desist in your efforts to collect on the debt account as stated above.

I would like to request, in writing, that no telephone contact be made by your offices to my home or to my place of employment. If your offices attempt telephone communication with me, including but not limited to computer generated calls and calls or correspondence sent to or with any third parties, it will be considered harassment and I will have no choice but to file suit. All future communications with me MUST be done in writing and sent to the address noted in this letter.

Yours truly,

Your Signature

Your Name

Once they get this letter they are bind by law to stop calling you. If they still call, they are breaking the law and you can sue them (and you should, it will costly only few bucks and it help you settle the debt) for up $1000 plus damages.

In addition to sending Cease and Desist letter you should also send them Debt Validation letter. This letter will prove that they are indeed bought your debt and are legally allowed to collect. (See sample below).

Your Name

Your Address

Your Phone #

Collector's Name

Collector's Address

Date

Dear Collection Manager,

Re: Account Number_____

This is to inform you that I've recently pulled my credit report and noticed that there's a collection from your agency on my credit report. I have never been notified of this collection. However, this letter does not imply that I refuse to pay this debt. Rather, I would like to dispute your claim.

As per the FDCPA, I have the right to request a validation of this debt. I request you to prove that I am indeed the party who is by contract obligated to pay off this debt.

I hope you are aware of the fact that reporting any invalidated information to major credit bureaus may constitute defamation of character, as negative listing on credit report does not allow me to enjoy the benefits of good credit. In addition, you must also be aware that until you validate this debt, you can neither continue collection activities nor report this information on my credit report. I'm sure your legal staff will agree that non-compliance with this request is likely to put your company in serious legal trouble with the Federal Trade Commission (FTC) and other state/federal agencies.

Please attach copies of the following documents:

1.Agreement with your client that authorizes you to collect on this alleged debt.

2.Agreement that bears signature of the alleged debtor wherein he promises to pay the creditor.

3.Complete payment history on this account so as to prove that the debt amount you wish to collect is correct.

With regards,

Your Signature

Your Name

You have to send this letter otherwise you could be end up paying or settling with somebody who has no legal right to your debt. And believe me there are hundreds CA and junk debt buyers who's only job is to call people every day and demand payment.

Actually demanding payment will probably be the first thing that collection agency asks you. Don't pay them anything. First send them a Cease and Desist letter and a Debt Validation letter. You send them this letter right after you received from them a debt validation notice. Under the Federal Law they have to send you this notice within five days after first contacting you over the phone. You have 30 days to send debt validation letter. If you do not send this letter CA has the right to assume that you own the debt. All letters to the collection agency should be sent not normal US mail, but certified return receipt requested so that you can verify with post office, if it was received and when and have the receipts in case you need to prove, that you sent them and diligently try to verify the debt. This is start of paper trail always keep a copy of these letters for yourself.

Even if you do own the debt they have to prove it and there is a chance that they do not have the proof and they will not be able to collect the debt. Look at the court decision from the case in Texas that I found online.

"John W argues that because <Collection Agency> did not submit a copy of the credit agreement signed by John W., < Collection Agency >did not prove the existence of an agreement or any of its terms.

< Collection Agency >did not produce the actual agreement or any other document that established the agreed terms, including the applicable interest rate or the method for determining the applicability and amount of finance charges. The interest rate and other information reflected in the statements that were provided by < Collection Agency >are inconsistent, varying from 5% to 22.4%, and there is no indication of the agreement reached as to interest.

Furthermore, < Collection Agency >presented no evidence on how it calculated the interest rates and finance charges that increased John W account balance from the $7,895.00 he owed on the June 2002 statement to the $14,153.90 < Collection Agency >claimed in its lawsuit.

While <Name Removed>summary judgment evidence might indicate that the parties had reached an agreement of some kind, their evidence is not sufficient to establish the terms of a valid contract as a matter of law. See John W, 232 S.W.3d at 202; T.O. Stanley Boot, 847 S.W.2d at 221.

Therefore, <Name Removed>did not meet its burden and summary judgment was inappropriate on <Name Removed>breach of contract theory. (5) See Knott, 128 S.W.3d at 215-16; John W, 232 S.W.3d at 202."

When CA buys debt from the original creditor they may or not buy all the documents regarding the debt. This is very expansive process. Each page goes for around $20. It simple not very cost effective for them to spend all the money to collect the debt.

After you send the Debt Validation letter the CA has 30 days to respond. The information that they send you back should include this:

- Document stating that they bought the debt or the debt is assigned to them from original creditor. This has to be official document. Hand written notes are not a proof.
- Original contract when you sign up for the credit card.
- Document showing your payment history on the account until now. Having this information will help you determine how much you owe and if the CA added any fess.

If they do not send you any information you have a right to refuse any payment. Send them again a copy of your original debt validation letter, copy of your mail receipt and a document stating that because they did not respond in timely manner they have violated the FDCPA and they can no longer collect the debt and they are not allowed to contact you.

Remember not to pay them anything until they can prove that this debt belongs to you. If you pay them, even a one dollar that will means that you acknowledge that this debt is yours and you are legally responsible for it. A lot of bad Collection agencies and debt buyers are counting on this. When they call you, they may say anything – legal or not – to make you pay.

Some will say; "We are going to garnish your wages if you don't pay" – Yes they can do that but only if the judge says so. And that means the have to sue you and win. And to win they have to behave and to prove that this debt is yours.

They may also say – and this is fairly common – that

"You will be arrested and send to jail if you do not pay immediately"

Or

"Sheriff Deputy will be at you house in 2 hours to take you to jail if you don't pay."

This is a lie. No one is going to arrest you, as owning a debt is civil matter not criminal one and no one can be sent to jail for not paying to the creditors. This is just a scare tactics they use and it's really nasty one and against the law.

"We will take your house away" – As long as you paying your mortgage and the debt is not secured by 2nd mortgage and home equity loan, no one will take your house.

They can also threat you with violence, call your neighbors, family members and tell them about your debt. Legally the only time they can call anyone other than you or your attorney is when they try to locate you. They are not allowed to say anything else.

Collection agencies and junk debt buyers are in business to make profit out of your debt so don't expect them to settle for less than 25% even if they bought the debt for 3 cent on the dollar. They don't actually tell you how much they paid for it, but they will demand that you pay 100% plus interest.

You know exactly how much you can pay so tell them that in the nicely letter you are going to send them but only after they sent you back the answer to your debt validation letter!

Send the settlement letter registered mail, return receipt. See below example. They will probably refuse at first or go down to 80%. Counter offer that with another letter stating that this is the only money you have and there is nothing

else you can do. They will probably suggest that you get a 2nd job. Yeah that's right, they don't care about you. Politely send another letter and another until you get the % you can afford.

If the collection agency did not respond to your debt validation letter and is ignoring your cease and desist letter and keeps calling you every day, file a complain with FTC and you State Attorney General.

The CA will then probably sell your debt to someone else or sue you. When they sue, you make sure you go to the court. The CA by suing you is actually counting on you not to show up, so they can get default judgment against you. And that would mean they won the case and they can now garnish your wages or levy your bank account.

But, if you go to the court you tell them that you neither admit nor deny anything until they showed you proof that they actually own your debt. You can also ask judge to dismiss the case because they did not validate the debt when you ask them to in your letter.

Collection agencies using their scare tactics prey on weak, unsuspecting people who are struggling to survive in bad economy. But once they realize that people are educated and aware of their rights they will start to play nicely and get the settlement that you want. Remember to track everything you do and what they do. If the violated the FDCPA sue them, they will be more willing to settle. You have a rights and knowledge is power. Knowledge may cost you some money but lack of knowledge will cost you more.

NEVER ADMIT IT IS YOUR DEBT UNTIL THEY CAN PROVE IT!

Part 7: Months and Years after settlement

Debt Scavengers

You successfully settled your debt and now you are free. Why are you then receiving phone calls telling you that you own some money?

Since the settled debt is on your credit report someone can get that information and sell it to junk debt buyer or debt scavenger. These people will simple call you and demand immediate payment or you will be send to jail, get arrested or sued. Don't fall for it, if you have your settlement terms in writing – and you should have - then you are fine. Do not pay them a dime. Ask them questions like who they are, where are they located, what is the balance, you can ask them for your name too. Most of the time they won't tell you any of that. Just simply tell them not to call you again and hung up. Some companies are notorious for doing that, calling people and hoping to score a payment. I did receive a call like that from "Jennifer"- very rude person – asking for payment. There are numerous cases where people were paying for months without seeing where the money goes or how much is there left to pay. Remember you only pay if the other party can prove that they are legally allowed to collect your debt.

Statue of Limitations

If you did not settle your debt and you were not sued – it happens - for period of 3-10 years – depending on the state where you live – you can no longer worry that you will be sued and required to pay the debt. So technically you could move abroad for few years and have the debt erased. For most of us this, however is not an option.

The purpose of SOL is to allow people not to worry of being sued for the rest of their life and be required to pay the debt. The creditor however still can sue you but if the Statue of Limitation expired they have no chance of winning the case. The reason they sue is they hope that you will be bullied in making payment and/or you do not go to the court and they can win by default. Just make sure you show up in the court and ask the judge to dismiss the case on ground that Statue of Limitations has expired. SOL is an ACTIVE-ONLY defense, that means you have to specifically tell the judge that SOL expired.

If someone will call you after all this years and demand payment on your old debt – do not get bullied and do not pay a dime. They cannot legally collect the debt and you have nothing to worry about. They will probably know that when they call, however they may use scare tactics to make you pay something promising that this is the last payment and you will never hear from them gain. Or that when you pay as little as $100.00 the will be able to settle the debt with you. This is a lie. If you pay as little as one dollar, you will make two things happen:

- You will reset Statue of Limitations to zero
- You will acknowledge that the debt is yours

And now whoever called has the right to collect he debt again. Do not fall for it! Here is a list of SOL for each state:

Statute of Limitation Chart				
State	Written Contracts	Oral Agreements	Promissory Notes	Open-ended Accounts
Alabama	6	6	6	3

Alaska	6	6	6	6
Arizona	6	3	5	3
Arkansas	5	3	6	3
California	4	2	4	4
Colorado	6	6	6	6
Connecticut	6	3	6	6
Delaware	3	3	6	3
D.C.	3	3	3	3
Florida	5	4	5	4
Georgia	6	4	6	4
Hawaii	6	6	6	6
Idaho	5	4	10	4
Illinois	10	5	6	5
Indiana	10	6	10	6
Iowa	10	5	5	5
Kansas	5	3	5	3
Kentucky	15	5	15	5
Louisiana	10	10	10	3
Maine	6	6	6	6
Maryland	3	3	6	3
Massachusetts	6	6	6	6
Michigan	6	6	6	6
Minnesota	6	6	6	6
Mississippi	3	3	3	3
Missouri	10	5	10	5
Montana	8	5	8	5
Nebraska	5	4	6	4
Nevada	6	4	3	4
New Hampshire	3	3	6	3
New Jersey	6	6	6	6
New Mexico	6	4	6	4
New York	6	6	6	6
North Carolina	3	3	5	3
North Dakota	6	6	6	6
Ohio	15	6	15	?

Oklahoma	5	3	5	3
Oregon	6	6	6	6
Pennsylvania	6	4	4	6
Rhode Island	15	15	10	10
South Carolina	10	10	3	3
South Dakota	6	6	6	6
Tennessee	6	6	6	6
Texas	4	4	4	4
Utah	6	4	6	4
Vermont	6	6	5	6
Virginia	5	3	6	3
Washington	6	3	6	3
West Virginia	10	5	6	5
Wisconsin	6	6	10	6
Wyoming	10	8	10	8

Here is interesting part. Some states have SOL shorter for oral than written contracts. So if you applied for the credit card over the phone or online, you could argue that SOL expired sooner and therefore you are protected against lawsuit.

Your Credit Score

Once all your debts are settled your credit score is low, but give it few months and it will start to go up. As I mention before your debt to income ratio has improved so you now have more buying power that the person that stills has thousands of dollars in credit card balance.

You can also do few other things you improve your credit

• Pay your other bills on time – duh!

- Get store card and used it wisely
- Get secured loan – you can secure the loan against your saving account.
- Get secured credit card – a card like that was my first ever credit card. It was issued by Citibank with $300 line of credit secured by $300 deposit.
- Do not use payday loans
- Pay your other bills on time – duh!

Credit score once ruined can be repaired so I'm not sure why everyone is making such a big deal out of it. Some people will tell you not to settle your debts or to declare bankruptcy because it will ruin your credit score. Well, with few thousands dollars in debt you can't do anything with you great credit anyway. My score was 720 but I couldn't get any new loan or buy anything because I was paying almost $1200 for my credit cards bill at high interest rate. That's right, although I had great credit (I was never late on the payment) I was charged 19%-24% interest rate just because the banks felt like it. More, everywhere you turn you heard that the credit score is the most important thing that you have to worry about! I'll tell you what is the most important:

- Making sure that your love one have something to eat
- Making sure that they have something to wear
- Making sure that they have a place to sleep

So instead paying my debt for the rest of my life I choose to damage my credit score and settle my debt. And right now, out of debt I can buy more things (with cash) because I no longer make minimum payments to my credit cards that was getting me nowhere.

Part 8: Debt Settlement and IRS

Believe it or not but settled debt is actually an income and surely you have to pay taxes. When your credit settles your debt, a savings of $600 or more off what you owed may be reported to by your creditor to the IRS and you will receive Form 1099-C. But here is a good thing:

You don't have to pay any tax if you are insolvent. In other words, if you would sell all of you assets (cars, jewelry, cloths, electronics, etc.) and you still would not have enough cash to pay all of your debts – you are insolvent.

Here is more info I took directly from IRS web site.

"Generally, if you owe a debt to someone and they cancel or forgive that debt, you are treated for income tax purposes as having in-come and may have to pay tax on this income"

"Example 1. In 2008, Greg was released from his obligation to pay his personal credit card debt in the amount of $5,000. Greg received a 2008 Form 1099-C from his credit card lender showing canceled debt of $5,000 in box 2. Greg uses the insolvency worksheet to determine that his total liabilities immediately before the cancellation were $15,000 and the FMV of his total assets immediately before the cancellation was $7,000. This means that immediately before the cancellation, Greg was insolvent to the extent of $8,000 ($15,000 total liabilities minus $7,000 FMV of his total assets). Because the amount by which Greg was insolvent immediately before the cancellation exceeds the amount of his debt canceled, Greg can exclude the entire $5,000 canceled debt from income.

When completing his tax return, Greg checks the box on line lb of Form 982 and enters $5,000 on line 2. Greg completes Part Ito reduce his tax attributes as explained under

Reduction of Tax Attributes, later. Greg does not include any of the $5,000 canceled debt on line 21 of his Form 1040. None of the canceled debt is included in his income."

Example 2. Assume the same facts as in Example 1 except that Greg's total liabilities immediately before the cancellation were $10,000 and the FMV of his total assets immediately before the cancellation was $7,000. In this case, Greg is insolvent to the extent of $3,000 ($10,000 total liabilities minus $7,000 FMV of his total assets) immediately before the cancellation. Because the amount of the canceled debt exceeds the amount by which Greg was insolvent immediately before the cancellation, Greg can exclude only $3,000 of the $5,000 canceled debt from income under the insolvency exclusion.

Greg checks the box on line lb of Form 982 and includes $3,000 on line 2. Also, Greg completes Part II to reduce his tax attributes as explained under Reduction of Tax Attributes, later. Additionally, Greg must include $2,000 of canceled debt on line 21 of his Form 1040 (unless another exception or exclusion applies).

Most of the people the time people who are in debt are insolvent and they will not pay any taxes. And even if you have to pay, that amount will be much smaller than your entire debt.

Last Word

Although I do believe that all debts should be paid, sometimes life can play some tricks on you and the creditors have to be satisfied will lesser amounts. Whether an illness, job loss, natural disaster or just a bad luck put you in debt, don't feel guilty for doing debt settlement. You have to do what is necessary to feed your family, provide a roof over their heads, cloths...

And banks... they will be all right. After all the 29% interest rate, numerous fees, or you, I mean the government will help them get on their feet.

Thank you

Thank you for buying this book. I hope it will help you be debt free.

I also would like to thank my creditors for accepting my settlement offers, especially the employees of Chase and Bank of America.

Thank you again!

www.ingramcontent.com/pod-product-compliance
Lightning Source LLC
Chambersburg PA
CBHW051248170526
45165CB00004B/1617